Historic Mill Creek Discovery Park

David A. Armour

STATE · HISTORIC · PARKS

Mackinac Island, Michigan

Historic Mill Creek Discovery Park
by: David A. Armour

Mackinac State Historic Parks
PO Box 370
Mackinac Island, Michigan 49757
MackinacParks.com

Printed in the United States of America

Revised edition 2019
First printing 3,000 copies

LEFT: Mill Creek winds through the park and under the sawmill.
RIGHT: Adventure Tour Guides lead visitors over the mill pond on the Forest Canopy Bridge.

Contents

LEFT AND BELOW: Demonstrations by costumed interpreters are a part of the experience at Mill Creek. Visitors can watch the water-powered saw in action as well as learn how logs were prepared before the mill was built. RIGHT: The Sugar Shack in the late winter as the maple tree sap begins to run.

Welcome to Historic Mill Creek Discovery Park!

THIS BEAUTIFUL PARK on the Straits of Mackinac beckons you to explore both the natural treasures of its 625 acres and the history which has taken place there, the site of Northern Michigan's first industrial complex. This book is for the first-time visitor as well as those who have visited the park before. If you have not yet walked Historic Mill Creek Discovery Park's forest trails or been fascinated by its operating, water-powered sawmill, we invite you to enjoy it all. If you are one of the thousands who have explored the park before, we hope this book sparks memories. Perhaps it will also acquaint you with a treasure you missed on an earlier visit.

Historic Mill Creek Discovery Park, opened in 1984, is one of the family of Mackinac State Historic Parks developed and operated by the Mackinac Island State Park Commission. (The commission invites you to visit its other sites as well: Colonial Michilimackinac and Old Mackinac Point Lighthouse in Mackinaw City and Fort Mackinac, the Mackinac Art Museum, and Mackinac Island State Park on Mackinac Island.)

In the David A. Armour Visitor's Center is a theater where an introductory audio-visual program is shown. The center also has a museum displaying many interesting objects excavated on the site, and a museum

shop offering books and other educational materials, as well as memorabilia, souvenirs, and light refreshments to enjoy at the nearby outdoor picnic tables or in the covered pavilion. Your visit will be greatly enhanced by spending time in the Visitor's Center at the start or finish of your visit to the park. Restrooms are located a few steps outside the Visitor's Center.

From the Visitor's Center it is only a short walk to the sawmill. You will pass the Forest Friends Play Area, a picnic area, the Water Power Station, the reconstructed millwright's house, and the Adventure Tour staging area. Take time to linger by the mill pond or stand on the bridge and listen to the water pouring over the dam. Sawmill demonstrations are signaled by the ringing of a large iron triangle. Demonstrations start at the saw-pit with hand-on participation by the audience. From the saw-pit, the interpreter moves to the sawmill to run the mill and cut a board. Following the inside demonstration, the guides lead the way outside where you can see the mill wheel in operation. Nearby is a barn-workshop which was reconstructed with wood sawn in the mill.

A popular way to learn about the park's natural history is to go on a naturalist-guided Adventure Tour. Sign up in the Visitor's Center, then meet your guide at the tour staging area near the mill pond, where you will get harnessed up for this exciting tour through the layers of the Mill Creek forest. Learn about the animals and plants that live on the forest floor and then travel through the forest understory into the trees while crossing the Forest Canopy Bridge. Fifty feet below this narrow suspension bridge Mill Creek flows into the mill pond. Be sure to pause on the bridge and discuss both the advantages and challenges that wildlife have when living in the trees.

The tour returns to the forest floor and continues along the stream, passing under the canopy bridge and crossing the stream on one of the park's several wooden bridges. Frequent stops are made to examine the flora and fauna of the forest and stream. The culmination of your tour is riding the Eagle's Flight Zip Line from the forest, down the stream and over the mill pond to where the tour

ABOVE: **Historic Mill Creek Discovery Park is pet friendly.** BELOW: **A U.S. soldier from Fort Mackinac lost this button at Mill Creek.**

began. Imagine you are a bald eagle gliding over the pond to catch a brook trout you saw from your perch in the trees.

Adventure Tour participants are also encouraged to climb the forty-foot-high climbing wall located on the side of the park's fifty-foot-high Treetop Discovery Tower. All park guests are welcome to take the stairs to the very top of the tower for a spectacular view of the Straits of Mackinac. The observation deck has a bench, several displays, and a telescope for a closer look at Mackinac Island

ABOVE: **In springtime male black-throated green warblers can be heard singing throughout the Mill Creek forest. RIGHT: Adventure Tour participants can climb up through the layers of the forest on the wall of the Treetop Discovery Tower.**

and the Mackinac Bridge. This is also a great place to observe the spring and fall migration of birds along the Straits of Mackinac.

You can reach the park's system of nature trails three ways. One is an accessible wooden ramp that leads from the Visitor's Center up the bluff to an overlook from which you can see Mackinac Island. Two routes provide access to the top on the sawmill side of the creek. One is a gravel path that follows an old logging trail. The other is a long, gradual, wooden ramp, which allows persons with disabilities, strollers or wheelchairs to use the trail system. The trail on the mill side leads to an active beaver dam about ½ mile upstream.

Trail maps are available at the Visitor's Center and additional maps are posted at trail junctions. Visitors should plan to spend at least an hour and a half at Historic Mill Creek Discovery Park, although many stay much longer so they can explore the park's many treasures more fully.

Groups are welcomed and special arrangements for programs or food service can be made.

LEFT: **A view of Mackinac Island from Historic Mill Creek Discovery Park.** RIGHT: **During thousands of years this small stream has cut a deepening valley as it makes its way to the lake.**

Geology and Land Forms

THE LAND AT HISTORIC MILL CREEK Discovery Park is constantly changing. The ground was formed over millions of years by colossal forces. Long ago, before the last great glaciers, the land was covered by a warm shallow ocean, and as small shells fell to the ocean floor, they gradually formed into layers of limestone rock. Eons later, the earth's climate cooled and mile-thick sheets of ice covered the land and scoured the bedrock.

As the climate warmed again, perhaps 10,000 years ago, the glaciers melted and the great wall of ice retreated northward, leaving behind dirt, rocks and other debris. Runoff from the melting glaciers eroded the land and formed a huge lake, which geologists call Lake Algonquin, that covered much of the upper Midwest. Its surface was more than 200 feet above the current Great Lakes and in the straits area only the very top of Mackinac Island rose above it.

The meltwater eventually carved an outlet, and as the water surged to the sea, it scoured a great trench in what are now the Straits of Mackinac. At first, the lake fell 350 feet, well below the current level. Then, slowly, the earth rebounded from the crushing weight of the glacier and a new lake, known as Lake Nipissing, formed about 5,000 years ago. Its surface was 25 feet higher than the present Lake Huron, and where it lapped the shore,

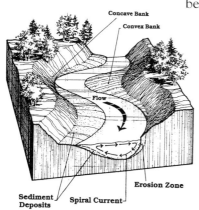

Concave Bank
Convex Bank
Flow
Erosion Zone
Sediment Deposits
Spiral Current

The moving water of Mill Creek is slowly but constantly changing the shape of its channel and the surrounding landscape.

it formed the terrace where the David A. Armour Visitor's Center and mill are. When water flowing out of Lake Nipissing eroded away an outlet where Port Huron is now, the surface fell to its present level, forming today's Lakes Huron and Michigan. Although these lake fluctuations happened thousands of years ago, they are very recent in terms of geological time.

Mill Creek, like most streams, was actually created by solar power. The sun evaporates the lake water, and the rising vapor cools and falls as rain and snow, which returns to the lake as a stream. Water falling on the land of Historic Mill Creek Discovery Park comes to earth 150 feet above Lake Huron where the underlying limestone and a layer of clay trap it to form Dingman Marsh. From there it flows back down Mill Creek to the lake. The limestone and clay create other, smaller wetlands on the plateau throughout the park. They are most pronounced along the trails on the east side of the creek.

Glacial Erratics Carried Up to 700 Miles

Ontario

Mill Creek

Michigan

LEFT AND BELOW: Huge rocks reveal the power of glaciers which cut the Great Lakes. Canadian boulders were lifted by the shifting ice and carried 700 miles southward to Michigan. As the glaciers receded, the boulders were left behind. RIGHT: Hikers on the Sugar Shack Forest Trail will find these fascinating specimens to study.

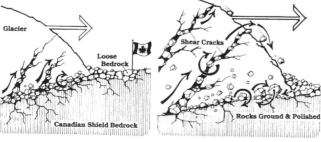

Glacier

Loose Bedrock

Canadian Shield Bedrock

Shear Cracks

Rocks Ground & Polished

Glacial Lake

Melt Water

Limestone

The Creek

MILL CREEK, THE OUTLET TO DINGMAN MARSH, is fed by seasonal runoff as well as small springs, and the amount of water flowing down the creek changes during the year. In January and February, when ice covers part of the creek, the flow is about two cubic feet per second. In April, melting snow and spring showers produce an annual peak of 18 cubic feet per second. Then in the dry summer months of July, August and September, the flow drops to only one cubic foot a second, although a thunderstorm might double or triple the flow for a day or two.

Stream flow is also regulated by control gates at the outlet of Dingman Marsh, but even when the gates are completely closed, small springs along the banks seep into the creek so that it never dries up.

Mill Creek drops farther than any other stream in the area of the Straits of Mackinac. Dingman Marsh is 730 feet above sea level and 150 feet above Lake Huron. Of the stream's total 150-foot drop, 120 feet are in the lower two miles, within the park boundary. The average drop of one foot for every 100 feet of creek is steep for a Michigan stream, and the resulting swift flow has

Spring run-off from melting snow brings the creek flow up to 18 cubic feet per second.

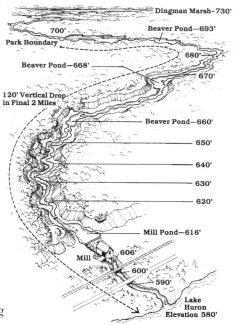

RIGHT: The swiftly flowing water of Mill Creek has cut a deep valley as it drops 150 feet to the lake. OPPOSITE RIGHT: The mill pond holds the creek flow to provide enough water to power the saw even when summer creek flows are reduced.

Dingman Marsh-730'

Beaver Pond—693'

700'

Park Boundary

680'

Beaver Pond—668'

670'

120' Vertical Drop in Final 2 Miles

Beaver Pond—660'

650'

640'

630'

620'

Mill Pond—616'

Mill

606'

600'

590'

Lake Huron Elevation 580'

cut a sharp valley through the plateau.

At a number of places Mill Creek is blocked by beaver dams, crudely but effectively engineered of sticks and mud. Some of the dams are maintained by active beaver colonies and form quiet pools. Other dams, abandoned, are slowly disintegrating under the relentless force of the water.

The cold stream provides a habitat for a wide variety of water creatures. Rainbow and brook trout lurk year-round in the riffles and eddies, and each spring suckers and smelt migrate upstream a short distance from Lake Huron to lay their eggs. To accommodate migrating fish, the reconstructed mill dam was built with a "fish ladder" beneath it that provides passage for fish when the dam is left open from late October until early May.

Painted turtles and frogs also live and breed in the stream. Frogs and toads lay their jelly-like clumps of eggs in the water, and after the tadpoles hatch, they develop legs and begin to breathe air from the surface. By the end of the summer most of the tadpoles have matured and left the water, but as adults they remain near the water's edge, feeding on insects. Many insects live at least part of their lives in the creek. Mosquitoes and black flies breed in the water and mayfly and stonefly nymphs forage for food on the rocky stream bottom. Diving beetles are common in the mill pond, and one can see the bubble of air each carries with it when swimming underwater. Water striders, light enough to take advantage of the surface tension of the water in ponds, skate on the surface, chasing mosquitoes.

Nature Notes

Northern White Cedar
Thuja occidentalis

- Prefers shallow, rich and moist soil.
- Can live to be over a thousand years old.
- Has fan-like branches and small scaly leaves.
- Winter food of the white-tailed deer.

The Forest

THE LAND AT HISTORIC MILL CREEK DISCOVERY PARK contains a variety of second-growth trees which have grown up since the forest was last logged more than 100 years ago. As you move inland from Lake Huron, the conifers (evergreen trees) give way to hardwoods. This is typical of forests along the edge of the northern Great Lakes; northern white cedar, balsam fir, white pine, white spruce and paper birch thrive in the cool, damp areas close to the lake and along the banks of Mill Creek itself. Cedar, especially, likes the moist ground along the creek and marsh. Near the base of the bluff is a transition zone where eastern hemlock and black ash are common. On the warmer, drier, inland plateau, such hardwoods as sugar maple, American beech and northern red oak predominate. In open areas created by forest fires, loggers or beavers, fast-growing quaking aspen trees are first to invade.

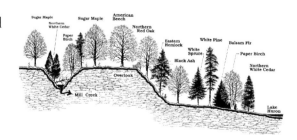

The forest at Historic Mill Creek Discovery Park is now mature, with several distinct layers of vegetation. The forest floor, understory and canopy each play an important role in the health of the forest and the lives of the animals that live there. The canopy, the highest layer of the forest, is formed by the branches and leaves of mature trees. It receives the most sunlight and is where most of the tree's food is made. The canopy forms a shady umbrella over the other layers. The middle understory is made of young trees and shade tolerant shrubs and bushes. Many trees in this layer will die before they reach full height. If an opening appears in the canopy, a few of the trees get more sunlight

which speeds their growth and they fill the gap. The forest floor is where dead plant and animal material is recycled into soil and where future understory and canopy plants begin life. Growing from the forest floor are ferns, grasses, mosses, mushrooms, wildflowers and tree seedlings. Animals that can not climb or fly live here. The different layers of the forest can be observed by climbing the Treetop Discovery Tower which begins on the forest floor and ends above the canopy.

To preserve the forest and interpret it for the enjoyment of the public, Historic Mill Creek Discovery Park has a forest management plan for perpetuating the natural resources and historic legacy of the site. There is no commercial timbering in the park. The plan's forest-management goals include:

- Maintaining a healthy and vigorous forest;
- Protecting water and soil resources;
- Creating and maintaining a variety of wildlife habitats;
- Providing timber for the water-powered sawmill;
- Providing demonstration areas for forest-management techniques;
- Educating and entertaining visitors.

Visitors can survey the Straits of Mackinac from the Treetop Discovery Tower.

LEFT: Adventure Tour participants cross the Forest Canopy Bridge 50 feet above Mill Creek. RIGHT: Visitors to the trails should take only pictures and leave only footprints.

Trails

NEARLY THREE MILES OF TRAILS allow visitors to explore Historic Mill Creek Discovery Park's forest and stream. Trails parallel the creek on both banks and cross it over four bridges, forming three major loops:

Loop 1, the "Mill Pond Trail," leads from the Visitor's Center to the mill dam, sawmill, and Treetop Discovery Tower, circling the main exhibit area and pond. It can be walked in about 15 minutes.

Along the Mill Pond Trail, near the top of the bluff, behind the Visitor's Center is the Forest Clearing. This is where park naturalists present natural history programs for visiting school groups in the spring and fall. Check at the visitor center for the daily schedule of special nature programs and hikes that begin in this cleaning.

Loop 2, the "Evergreen Trail," winds along the cool forest at the top of the bluff. At places along the way, hikers can glimpse the creek where it is still cutting through the ancient limestone bedrock. Walking time is 25 minutes.

Farther down the trail, just past the beginning of the Evergreen Trail is the Sounds of the Forest Discovery Station. This is an ideal spot to experience and learn about the variety of sounds that can be heard in the Mill Creek forest.

Loop 3, the "Beaver Pond Trail," overlooks the lodges of several industrious beaver families. Hikers are occasionally rewarded with a glimpse of these shy creatures. Walking time is approximately 60 minutes.

In addition, two side-loops of about half a mile each allow visitors to explore other areas of the forest. Each can be walked in about 15 minutes. One, the "Aspen-Wildlife Forest Trail," goes through the park's aspen forest and demonstrates aspen management techniques. Aspen is a fast-growing, short-lived tree that is a valuable source of commercial pulpwood and an important source of food and

TRAIL MAP

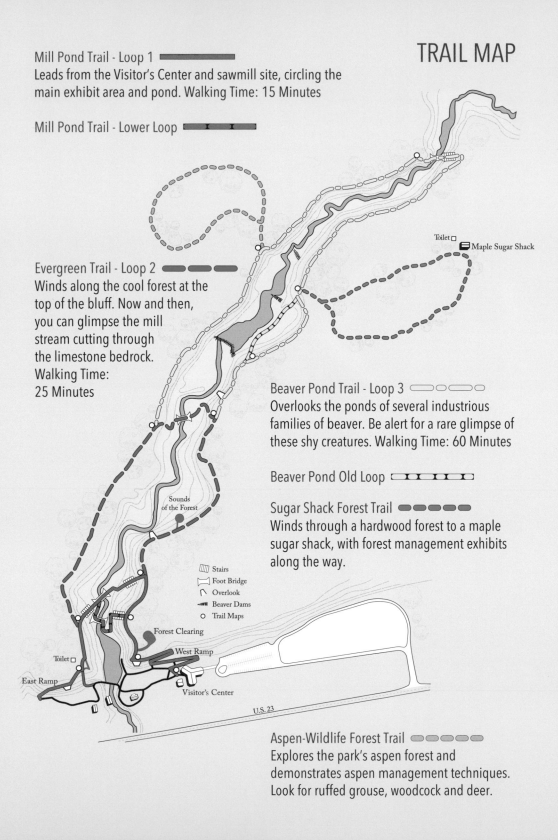

Mill Pond Trail - Loop 1
Leads from the Visitor's Center and sawmill site, circling the main exhibit area and pond. Walking Time: 15 Minutes

Mill Pond Trail - Lower Loop

Evergreen Trail - Loop 2
Winds along the cool forest at the top of the bluff. Now and then, you can glimpse the mill stream cutting through the limestone bedrock. Walking Time: 25 Minutes

Beaver Pond Trail - Loop 3
Overlooks the ponds of several industrious families of beaver. Be alert for a rare glimpse of these shy creatures. Walking Time: 60 Minutes

Beaver Pond Old Loop

Sugar Shack Forest Trail
Winds through a hardwood forest to a maple sugar shack, with forest management exhibits along the way.

Aspen-Wildlife Forest Trail
Explores the park's aspen forest and demonstrates aspen management techniques. Look for ruffed grouse, woodcock and deer.

Toilet

Maple Sugar Shack

Sounds of the Forest

Stairs
Foot Bridge
Overlook
Beaver Dams
Trail Maps

Forest Clearing

West Ramp

Toilet

East Ramp

Visitor's Center

U.S. 23

RIGHT: Well marked trails invite exploration. BELOW: Marsh marigolds are among the many wildflowers hikers can observe along the trail.

shelter for deer, beaver, ruffed grouse, and other wild animals.

The "Sugar Shack Forest Trail" winds through a beautiful, northern, hardwood forest to a reconstructed maple-sugar shack from the early 1900s. Although the forest is primarily sugar maple, it includes beech, oak, basswood, ash, hemlock, and other species. Along the way are several exhibits showing aspects of forest management commonly used in Michigan's hardwood forests.

Also, along the forest trails are approximately 50 displays to acquaint the hiker with unique features of the forest and landscape, and 20 smaller Nature Notes identifying species of trees and shrubs.

Here are some guidelines to help you enjoy the trails:
- Walk quietly
- Experience the forest with your eyes, ears, and nose
- Take your time and you will see more
- Stay on marked trails to avoid getting lost
- Do not pick or damage any plants
- Keep pets leashed to protect wildlife
- Deposit litter in a trash receptacle

Remember that Historic Mill Creek Discovery Park is "home" to wildlife and that you are a guest.

LEFT: **The long-eared owl is just one of the owls that call the Historic Mill Creek Discovery Park forest home.** RIGHT: **Porcupines come out at night to chew on the park's buildings.**

Wildlife

THE FIRST ANIMALS VISITORS MEET at Historic Mill Creek Discovery Park are likely to be lively chipmunks that scurry around the picnic shelter area looking for handouts. Porcupines come to the shelter at night to chew on the building's plywood, because they like the taste of the glue in it. Rose-breasted grosbeaks, cardinals, black-capped chickadees, blue jays, white-breasted nuthatches, and goldfinches bustle around the bird feeders outside the Visitor's Center window, and ruby-throated hummingbirds dart in to suck sweet liquid from other feeders. Ducks and Canada geese occasionally land on the mill pond, where belted kingfishers dive into the water after prey.

The park is home to many wild creatures. At the Visitor's Center, mounted birds and animals invite close inspection.

White-tailed deer are occasionally seen in the park, although in summer they usually feed at night and bed down during the day. Deer often visit the stream for water in late afternoon, leaving tracks behind in the damp soil. The deer's summer diet includes acorns, apples, grasses, mushrooms, and strawberries. When deep snow covers the forest, deer congregate in the swamps, where the foliage of the white cedar becomes their major winter food source.

Many deer make their home in the Historic Mill Creek Discovery Park area. Visitors might only catch a glimpse of them at dusk but can watch for their tracks along the trails.

The park's hardwood forest provides food and shelter for a variety of animals – deer mice, woodpeckers, porcupines, and black bears. Forest management techniques make this area attractive to wildlife by increasing the diversity of foliage. Limited timber harvesting makes small clearings where shrubs and ground cover can flourish. Trees that produce acorns, fruits and nuts are also encouraged, and brush piles built to provide shelter for small creatures. Den trees and some dead trees are left standing, and nest boxes are provided for squirrels, woodpeckers, and owls.

Fallen trees provide food and shelter for a variety of creatures. When an old tree falls, the important process of returning nutrients to the soil begins. A succession of plants and animals invade the log. First come fungi, mosses, lichens, termites, and wood-boring beetles. Besides breaking down the log into soil they attract predatory animals such as carpenter ants, centipedes, salamanders, woodpeckers, chipmunks, raccoons, and skunks. While searching for food, many of these predators dig or tunnel into the log. Some make it their home.

Scattered throughout the forest, sinkholes in the limestone create an unusual environment for certain plants and animals. The sinkholes are created when water dissolves

underlying limestone layers to the point that the overlying limestone collapses. Such holes vary in size and shape. Sinkholes provide a moist, shaded environment that is ideal for many species of mosses and ferns. Garter snakes find sinkholes an excellent place to hibernate

ABOVE: **An abandoned beaver pond.** RIGHT: **The beaver plays a significant role in creating the landscape along Mill Creek.**

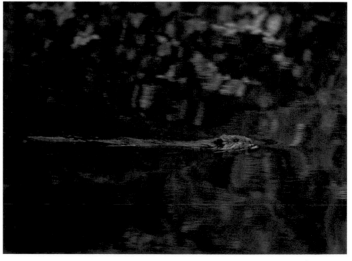

BELOW: Beavers construct their dams to provide both food and shelter. The dam forms a pond, which creates a constant store of food.

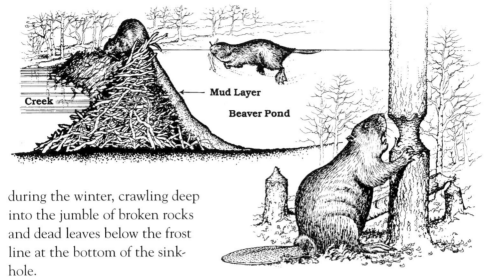

Creek

Mud Layer

Beaver Pond

during the winter, crawling deep into the jumble of broken rocks and dead leaves below the frost line at the bottom of the sink-hole.

The animal that has made the most dramatic impact on the Mill Creek landscape is the beaver, the largest rodent in North America. During its 10 to 15 years of life an average adult beaver, weighing from 30 to 60 pounds, changes the forest environment more than any other animal in the north woods. Beavers use their massive front teeth to cut down aspen trees. They build dams across streams by laying down hundreds of sticks and packing them with mud and rocks from the stream bottom. The dams turn narrow, swift streams into wide, slow-moving marshes and ponds. The trees they cut can be two feet in diameter, and beavers can turn dense forest into open meadow.

A beaver colony has built a series of dams along Mill Creek. Beavers usually work at night but are sometimes seen swimming across the pond during the day by people who are quiet, patient, and a bit lucky.

Beavers live in family "colonies" of up to 12 members. A typical colony consists of two breeding adults, yearlings born the previous year and two to six kits born in the current year. Beavers frequently construct a lodge of sticks and mud to serve as their winter home, where they remain safe and warm when ice covers the pond. They make several underwater entrance tunnels, and swim out under the ice only to reach their submerged food cache. Not all beavers live in lodges. Some dig underwater tunnels into the pond bank leading to an underground den built just above water level.

LEFT: A staff naturalist explains how we can help wildlife both in the park and back home. BELOW: The beaver lodge is a complex structure that uses the water to protect the beavers from land-based predators. RIGHT: The beaver ponds are among Mill Creek's richest habitats.

The habitat created by beavers attracts many other types of wildlife. Deer, snowshoe hares, and ruffed grouse visit the sunny new forest openings to feed on the aspen shoots that flourish in them. Wood ducks, belted kingfishers, and tree swallows build their nests above or near the beaver pond. Frogs, turtles and water snakes search for food in and around the pond. They, in turn, are hunted by raccoon, mink, and great blue herons.

After the readily available food around one pond has been harvested, the beaver abandon their pond and move on to make a new dam. Without the beavers to make repairs, the dam slowly disintegrates and the pond drains. Grasses and wildflowers such as cardinal flower and Joe Pye weed quickly move to form a stream-cut meadow. Shrubs and trees such as speckled alder follow rapidly and turn the old pond site back into forest.

Eventually the combination of running water and new trees attracts another beaver colony, and the cycle starts again.

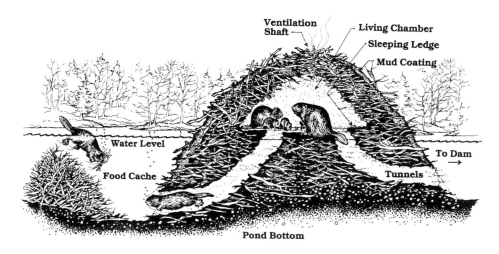

Mill Creek Rediscovered

ONE SUMMER DAY IN 1972 Margaret Lentini and Ellis and Mary Olson, amateur archaeologists from Cheboygan, came to Mill Creek with a metal detector to search for a mill they knew had once been there. Ellis Olson had seen some old millstones in people's backyards in Cheboygan, and his research indicated they had originally come from Mill Creek. What he didn't know was just where the mill was or what it was like.

Searching was not easy because thick brush covered the stream banks, but several hewn logs in the stream indicated clearly where a dam had once been. As they searched along the high east bank downstream from the dam, the metal detector gave a distinctive ping. Digging carefully, they found several items including a flintlock musket lock and several pieces of thin brass decorated with a lion and a crown.

Ellis Olsen took the objects to Dr. Lyle Stone, staff archaeologist of the Mackinac Island State Park Commission, who then was excavating at Fort Michilimackinac in Mackinaw City. Dr. Stone recognized the pieces of brass as being from the hat of a British soldier of the War of 1812 period. Stone showed the artifacts to Dr. David Armour, deputy director of the Mackinac Island State Park Commission, who realized that the cap plate had come from a soldier at Fort Mackinac, which the Park Commission had been restoring since 1958. Excited by the new find, Dr. Armour authorized an exploratory excavation at Mill Creek.

The test excavations revealed a depression in the ground that had been a storage basement, and a mound of dirt which covered a stone fireplace. They also yielded ceramic sherds and other objects from the late 1700s or early 1800s,

ABOVE: Excavation at the Millwright's House during the 1980's.
RIGHT: The white chalk lines outline the Millwright's House.

including military buttons from Fort Mackinac. The site had an air of mystery about it. Close inspection of the few early maps of the straits revealed a mill on the stream, but none of the maps showed the exact location. Historical documents were also sketchy.

While searches for additional maps and records were

begun in a number of libraries and archives, further archaeological excavation was clearly needed to learn more about the history of Mill Creek. The site begged to be explored. With permission of the Department of Natural Resources Forestry Division (which held title to the land), the Park Commission sent a small archaeological crew to conduct excavations during the summers of 1973, 1974, and 1975 under the direction of Patrick Martin, a Michigan State University graduate student.

Martin and his team located the remains of two substantial houses, one on each side of the creek, as well as the remains of a barn on the east bank. They mapped the locations of the logs from the dam and dug test pits over a large area in an attempt to locate the site of the mill.

The archaeological evidence indicated there had been a substantial community at Mill Creek from approximately 1780 to 1840, and that the community was closely connected to Fort Mackinac and Mackinac Island. Believing that the area might have potential for development as a historic park, the Mackinac Island State Park Commission requested that the Michigan Legislature transfer the 503-acre site from the Forestry Division to the Park Commission. In 1975 the transfer was made.

Because there are so few maps and historical documents relating to Mill Creek, archaeology has been the most important source of information about this site and its inhabitants. Archaeologists excavated periodically from 1972 until 1994. Their goal was to discover how people used this site.

Before the archaeologists began digging, what was known about the site had come from local lore, historical records and documents, including the knowledge that an enterprising Scotsman Robert Campbell built a mill on Mill Creek in the 1780s, during the American Revolution.

BELOW: **Campbell cut large quantities of hay at his farm. This scythe blade was used and repaired at the site.**

Millstone

These granite millstones are a pair that legend states came from Mill Creek.

Robert Campbell had added a gristmill to his sawmill operation at Mill Creek by the early 1800s. In 1860, twenty years after the mill was abandoned, the stones were obtained by James Myers for use in his mill in nearby Cheboygan. He transferred the stones to his Myers Creek Mill south of town in the middle 1860s. The mill ceased operation by 1890.

In 1968 one of the stones, now broken, was found at the Myers' mill site by local historian Ellis Olson, who later donated it the Mackinac Island State Park Commission. The discovery further compelled him to search for the forgotten Mill Creek site.

But what happened to the second stone? Apparently, in the early 1890s the other stone was acquired by Walter Watson, a local farmer. It was taken by raft from Myers Creek down the Cheboygan River to the Watson farm south of Cheboygan. Watson intended shipping it to the World's Colombian Exposition in Chicago. It never made it to the fair but remained on the Watson farm for the next century. In 1994 his granddaughter, Florence Bradstrom, donated the second stone to the commission. Both stones are now exhibited at the site.

LEFT: A visitor is recruited to help an interpreter demonstrate pit sawing. **RIGHT AND BELOW:** Along with the Mill Creek millstones, Robert Campbell's will is the only original non-archaeological artifact from the Mill Creek site discovered to date. Among other provisions, the will specifies that the mill goes to his son John.

Robert Campbell's Mill

ROBERT CAMPBELL WAS THE FIRST to recognize Mill Creek's potential for powering a mill. He came to the Straits of Mackinac from his native Scotland to seek his fortune in the fur trade, sometime after the British took control of the French fort in 1761.

In those days, keeping warm in winter meant burning prodigious amounts of wood in fireplaces. Each winter every fireplace consumed 15 cords, the equivalent of a woodpile four feet high, four feet wide, and 120 feet long. Both for firewood and to get timbers for construction, wood cutters from Michilimackinac harvested the trees close to shore and transported the wood by boat to the fort. By the late 1700s much of the forest along the lake between Fort Michilimackinac and the creek had been cut down. Most, however, was used without being sawn into boards.

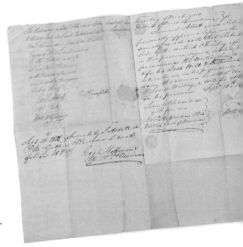

During the American Revolution, in 1779-1781, there was a sudden boom in demand for sawn lumber, when the British, afraid of an American attack, decided to move the fort and town from the mainland to Mackinac Island.

Without a sawmill, every board had to be sawn laboriously by hand. The usual method in those days required two men. The log was either raised on tall sawhorses, or above a deep pit in the ground. The "tiller man" stood on top of the log, directing the saw blade and hauling it up after each stroke. The "pit man" stood under the log and pulled down on the saw. The saw cut only on the down-

RIGHT: This "stubshot" was found on Mackinac Island. BELOW: This diagram of a "stubshot" shows how the logs were first squared, then sawn and finally cut off into separate boards at the construction site. OPPOSITE RIGHT: This drawing of a colonial sawmill in New York is similar to Campbell's mill.

stroke, and the pit man got the sawdust in his face. Working all day, two men could cut perhaps 14 boards, 20 feet long. It was exhausting work.

With a water powered mill to drive a similar up-an-down blade, the same men could cut 150 boards in a day with much less effort. The key would lie in finding a stream that could be dammed to provide enough water falling a sufficient distance to provide the power to drive a mill. Robert Campbell recognized that in the straits area only Mill Creek had enough of a fall to generate the necessary power, and that by damming it he could obtain enough waterpower to drive a small sawmill.

Campbell obtained use of 640 acres along the southeast side of the British military reservation surrounding Fort Michilimackinac, land the Indians had granted to the British. Campbell never received a formal deed, however. The building boom on Mackinac Island during the 1780s kept Campbell busy sawing boards in those seasons when there was enough stream flow to permit the mill to operate.

Campbell used horses and oxen to drag the heavy logs to the mill. Before sawing boards, Campbell would usually square the log first with a broad axe. When the mill ripped the log into boards, it sawed all but the last few inches.

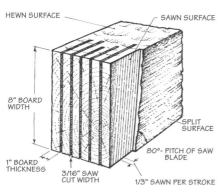

HEWN SURFACE — SAWN SURFACE
8" BOARD WIDTH
SPLIT SURFACE
1" BOARD THICKNESS
3/16" SAW CUT WIDTH
80°- PITCH OF SAW BLADE
1/3" SAWN PER STROKE

The unsawn end, called a "stubshot," kept the boards together to simplify transporting them to Mackinac Island. The sawn logs were dragged by oxen to the shore, where they were rafted together with chains and floated across to the island. Only when the logs reached the job site were the boards sawn off to release them from the stubshot end of the log.

From subsequent excavation, we have

learned that Campbell built a two-room log house near his mill on the east side of the creek, heated by a two-sided fireplace between the rooms. Nearby he erected a workshop-storehouse from boards sawn in the mill. Fields cleared of trees were planted to provide hay and pasturage for the horses and oxen. Campbell was as much a farmer as a sawmill operator, and he probably continued to trade with the Indians for furs as well.

At the conclusion of the American Revolution in 1783, the Straits of Mackinac became part of the new nation, whose flag first waved over Mackinac Island in 1796 when the American army came to garrison the fort. Campbell, like many others then living at the straits, had no papers to show ownership of the land on

which he was living. But if he was anxious, he was soon relieved to learn that at the Treaty of Greenville in 1795, the local Chippewa chief had reconfirmed the Indians' grant of the land on which his mill stood.

By the early 1800s Campbell's farm, as it was known, included several buildings, 40 acres under cultivation, a large orchard, and a grist mill as well as the sawmill. The grist mill, with its large, granite grinding stones, had been added to grind corn and other grains. Much of the corn came from distant Indians, since little land was cultivated in the straits area.

When Robert Campbell died in 1808, his 22-year-old son, John, took over the mill. Among the historical records available concerning the mill are a map and a land claim. The claim was filed with the Detroit Land Office by Robert's heirs after his death, to secure firm title to their inheritance. The land claim was confirmed because the heirs proved Campbell had occupied the lands prior to 1796, the year the United States took jurisdiction. The map was drawn in 1810 by Deputy Surveyor Aaron Greeley. After surveying the straits area that year, he indicated the Campbell property on his map as "Private Claim 334."

After having secured the title, Campbell's heirs decided to sell the property, and in 1819 they found a buyer in the person of Michael Dousman, a wealthy Mackinac merchant.

Michael Dousman's Mill

MICHAEL DOUSMAN, BORN IN PITTSBURGH IN 1771, came to Mackinac in 1796, soon after the American takeover, and became active in the fur trade. Dousman acquired considerable property in the area, including a farm of several hundred acres on the north end of Mackinac Island.

When the British attacked Mackinac Island in the summer of 1812, they captured Dousman, but let him warn civilians on the island to get out of harm's way before fighting began. Some people later called Dousman a traitor because he remained on Mackinac during the British occupation and sold supplies to the garrison. Dousman, however, was able to prosper even in adversity, and he enlarged his fortune through the fur trade even as he defended his reputation. By the 1820s, he was the second largest property holder in Michilimackinac County.

Part of his estate was the mill and farm which he had purchased in 1819 from the heirs of Robert Campbell, including John Campbell and his wife, Elizabeth. Dousman, who lived on the island, sent an employee to live at Mill Creek and manage the farm and operate the mill. The census of 1820 listed 24 persons in Dousman's household, which included the people who worked for him. Some of them undoubtedly lived at Mill Creek, but we do not know their names.

By that time, Robert Campbell's original log house on the east side of the creek had burned down, and Dousman's men erected a new structure west of the creek. Excavation shows it to have measured 17 by 40 feet and to have consisted, as did Campbell's, of two rooms divided by a double fireplace. The western room served as living quarters.

The eastern room, occupying about one-third of the house, served as a workshop and forge. Porches along the north and south sides of the house commanded a view of the straits to Mackinac Island.

Today this structure has been reconstructed on its original site. Costumed interpreters used lumber sawn at the mill and period tools and techniques to construct the exterior of the building. Inside, visitors can view the remains of the original double-sided fireplace and root cellar. The original millstones and artifacts found during the excavation of the house are on display in modern museum exhibits.

Under Dousman's ownership the mill continued to saw boards for use on Mackinac Island, some of it from logs rafted across to Mill Creek from nearby Bois Blanc Island. During the 1820s Mackinac Island's fur trade, dominated by John Jacob Astor's American Fur Company, was at its peak, and the growing community meant steady demand for building materials. The mill sold lumber to the U.S. Indian agent and to others who built the Mission House (1825) and the Mission Church (1829) on Mackinac Island.

By the mid-1830s, however, the fur trade was in decline. The mill ceased operation in 1839. There was a flicker of hope that the economy at Mill Creek might revive when government surveyors designated it as the northern terminus of a proposed road from Saginaw to Mackinac. After some clearing of land for the road, however, the project died, and the area began to revert to wilderness.

THIS PAGE: **Plan of Historic Mill Creek Discovery Park** shows the reconstructed buildings as they may have looked in Michael Dousman's time as well as showing the current Visitor's Center, Adventure Tour and trail system.
OPPOSITE PAGE: **The reconstructed American Millwright's House showcases original ruins of the structure and modern museum exhibits.**

New Owners

WHEN MICHAEL DOUSMAN DIED in 1854, his heirs sold Private Claim 334 to William W. Wendell for a mere $400. The only visitors there were surveyors and a few fishermen.

Shortly after the Civil War a tenant of Wendell's, a man named Young, built a house on the property and quarried limestone for a couple of years. Later, Wendell rented the house to Charles Bennett and his wife Angeline, who lived there from about 1870 until 1910. The Bennett's served as caretakers of the property until the house burned about 1910. During their stay, portions of the property were leased to the Petoskey Mackinaw Lime Co., which extracted limestone and clay, probably for local road-building. Evidence of the quarry operation is still visible in places along the stream and the bluff. The quarrying may have destroyed the site of the original mill, although it did not touch the dam.

In 1881 the Detroit and Mackinac Railroad Company built a track along the shore of Lake Huron that bridged the creek a few yards downstream from the site of the dam and mill. Workers building the line found a small brass or copper plaque bearing the inscription:

> *Here lieth the Body of*
> *John Annan Late Corpl*
> *In the 2nd Battn 60th Regt*
> *who departed this lif feby 10*
> *Anno Domini 1771*
> *Aged 51 years.*

British muster rolls from Fort Michilimackinac confirm that John Annan did indeed die on that day, perhaps while on a wood-cutting detail.

TOP: **One of the most recognizable summer flowers at Mill Creek is the yellow lady's slipper.** RIGHT: **This ca. 1915 photo shows limestone quarrying at the site.**

The rail line operated until the late 1980s, then was abandoned and its rails pulled up. It is now the North Central State Trail, a multi-use recreational trail.

Only a few feet downstream from the dam a bridge was erected early in the 20th century for the Old Mackinaw Trail highway to cross the creek. The abutment is still there. When this road, now U.S. 23, was rebuilt nearer the lake, the Old Mackinaw Trail road was abandoned, but part of its route is now followed by the exit road from the park.

Over the years Private Claim 334 has been divided into several parcels. During the Depression, 503 acres reverted to the state when the owners could not pay their property taxes. That's how the property came into the hands of the Conservation Department's Forestry Division. There it remained, administered as part of Mackinaw State Forest and guarding the secrets of its past, until Ellis Olson's discoveries led to the extensive archaeological and reconstruction efforts of the Mackinac State Park Commission.

LEFT: **Historic Mill Creek Discovery Park was heavily wooded when archaeology began.** RIGHT: **This brass wedding ring was lost by someone who lived in the Millwright's House.** BELOW: **This serpent sideplate from a flintlock trade musket is one of many artifacts uncovered at Historic Mill Creek Discovery Park.**

Archaeology at Historic Mill Creek

THE PARK IS HEAVILY WOODED and covered with thick brush, and in summer, foliage blocks the view more than few feet ahead. Consequently, archaeological features were not found quickly. More may remain to be discovered, hidden by the leaves and brush.

Archaeologists must work carefully and methodically and keep thorough records. They first survey the site into 10-foot squares, giving each square a number. As they dig, they record the square, and the exact location within it, where each archaeological feature and artifact is found. Furthermore, the depth at which something is found is carefully recorded. This provides a clue to the age of an artifact, since older objects are normally found in lower layers.

Each building or structure unearthed is also given a number to indicate that everything found within its boundaries is related. By 1994, five structures had been found at Historic Mill Creek Discovery Park.

In 1972, when investigation began, the most obvious objects visible were some of the logs of the dam, which remained in their original position across the creek. Subsequent excavation revealed that the dam was constructed as a crib of interlocked cedar timbers filled with large stones. The ends of the dam were keyed into limestone bedrock on each side of the stream. The upstream side of the dam was sheeted with boards, some of which survived and are on display in the museum. The boards were placed on a slant so that the dam was much wider at its base than at the top. By noting where the dam joined the banks, archaeologists could determine where its crest was and, from that calculate the size of the mill pond. That helped them judge where below the dam the mill might have been, because for a sawmill to operate efficiently, water must drop at least 10 feet onto the water wheel.

The search for the sawmill was frustrating. Numerous test pits between the dam and the lake revealed nothing. Finally archaeologists concluded that the mill site had been either destroyed by the limestone quarrying operation or had been built in the creek on stilts which left no trace. Although archaeologists failed to find the mill structure, they did find part of the saw blade. This treasure revealed the blade's thickness and the size and shape of the saw teeth.

On the east side of the creek the first building found is also the oldest. Known as Structure One, it is the house Robert Campbell built, a log building 40 feet by 20 feet, situated perpendicularly to the stream with its western wall close to the bank. The sill logs were laid on a prepared clay base. The walls were laid horizontally, mortised into vertical posts and chinked with clay. Plaster had been applied on the inside to make the house weather-tight. A stone chimney in the center of the building has two fireplaces facing in opposite directions into the two rooms of the house. The hearth base is 6 by 10 feet and two feet high. The scattering of stones nearby indicates that the chimney probably rose six or eight feet. The top of the chimney was probably of wood lined with clay, a common method in those days in the upper Great Lakes. Beneath the wooden floor of the western room was a storage cellar five feet deep and measuring 14 feet north to south and 9 feet east to west. Such cellars kept food cool in summer.

Archaeologists found evidence that the building had burned down.

Artifacts found in the Campbell House, such

ABOVE: Each site is excavated in layers, revealing the stone fireplaces and building foundations. LEFT: A horse shod with this shoe dragged logs to the mill and plowed the fields.

as broken ceramics, buttons, bottles and straight pins, identify the building as a residence. The type of ceramics indicates the building was occupied from the late 1700s until the early 1800s. It was on the site of this house that Cheboygan's amateur archaeologists found the musket flintlock and British brass cap late in 1972.

Structure Two, the British Workshop, is immediately east of, and at right angles to, the Campbell House. It has a very different construction and function.

It was a frame building on blocks of stone. Very few domestic objects were found there, but tools and other items suggest a storehouse and workshop.

Structure Three, the Millwright's House, resembles the Robert Campbell House, but has a distinct difference. Located on the west side of the creek, it was also perpendicular to the creek and built of squared logs with dovetailed corners. It measured 40 by 17 feet and was plastered on the inside. A central fireplace and chimney divided it into two rooms. The western room was the living quarters, under whose plank flooring a 5 by 7-foot storage cellar was dug. The room nearer the creek contained a fireplace but was largely sand-floored. The sand contained charcoal, slag, corroded iron and scrap metal, rivets and tools, marking it as a workshop where iron objects were heated and worked.

U.S. military buttons dating from the 1790s to the 1820s reveal continuing contact with Fort Mackinac on Mackinac Island. Artifacts from the house indicate that it was occupied from about 1820 to the 1840s and that the occupants were of medium economic position. The family ate a lot of meat from cows, pigs, and chickens as well as wild animals, birds, and fish. Someone could read and write because a lead pencil was found. A man of the house used a straight razor blade. The discovery of small buttons, necklace beads and sewing implements suggest a woman's presence as well. One of the most poignant discoveries was a brass wedding ring, decorated with two entwined hearts. It must have caused considerable distress when it was lost through a crack in the floor.

Several unusual items were found in the house. One, an 1805 Irish commemorative coin celebrating Field Marshal Wellington, suggests that the family in the house was Irish. Another unusual object found there is a Haitian military button. Pictured on it is a phoenix with spread wings over the regiment number "29". Encircling the rim is the motto *Je Renais de Mes Cendres* (I am reborn from my ashes). Haitian soldiers never came to Mill Creek, but similar buttons found on other archaeological sites were a popular trade item with the Indians during the 1830s. Many of these artifacts are on display in the reconstructed house.

Sites of two other structures have also been found, but have not yet been thoroughly examined. Both are on the east side of the creek between the Old Mackinaw Trail and the bluff, and are visible as raised mounds on the ground. They appear to be from late 19-century or early 20th-century structures. One, a rectangle of 75 by 20 feet, appears to have been a barn or shed. The other, a 15-foot circle, might be a silo.

ABOVE: Buried beneath several feet of silt, these boards from the upstream side of the dam survived for nearly 200 years. OPPOSITE: Haitian soldiers never came to Mackinac, but their buttons were popular items for trade with the Native Americans.

LEFT: The interpreters, using period tools and authentic methods, have provided labor for many reconstruction projects, both small and large. RIGHT: Work on the Millwright's House reconstruction began in the summer of 1995.

Money and Manpower

AFTER THE EARLY EXPLORATION following the 1972 discoveries, a grant was secured in 1977 from the National Endowment for the Humanities to assess the development potential of the site. Victor Hogg, a museum designer, headed a planning team that developed a master plan for blending historic reconstruction with interpretation of natural resources to tell the story of the site from the Ice Age to the present. Impressed by the plan, the Mackinac Island State Park Commission authorized the staff to seek further grants to implement it. Coastal Zone Management of the U.S. Department of Commerce, the Upper Great Lakes Regional Commission, and the Land and Water Conservation Fund provided $200,000 in grants.

This allowed additional excavation in 1979 and 1980 by archaeologist Tom Ford, as well as reconstruction of the dam and construction of the nature trails.

In 1982 the Park Commission issued $500,000 in revenue bonds to develop Historic Mill Creek State Park and open it as a park to the public. A replica of the water-powered sawmill was built, as were the Visitor's Center with its museum and theater areas, and the restroom-picnic shelter building. Hogg fabricated

the museum exhibits and Jeffrey Dykehouse, a staff naturalist with the Park Commission, developed an audio-visual program. The park opened on June 15, 1984.

Before the park opened it was recognized for its value as a natural area. Early development plans included construction of the nature trails.

Since opening the park, the commission has

continued to develop and expand it. Additional lands from Private Claim 334 have been purchased, bringing the park to its present 625 acres. Archaeologists completed excavating the Millwright's House on the west bank, providing sufficient information for reconstruction. Today you can walk through the reconstruction and see the original double fireplace and root cellar, artifacts found during excavation, and the original stones from the grist mill. Costumed interpreters have reconstructed the barn-workshop, using historic tools and wood sawn in the mill. The trail system has been expanded, including the Adventure Tour, and improved, with better surfaces and ramps on both sides of the creek to make the nature trails more accessible. Interpretive exhibits and the sugar-making shack have been added. A naturalist, hired with funds from the Mackinac Associates friends organization, enhances the natural-history programs, especially for school groups.

ABOVE AND LEFT: **Costumed interpreters built the barn-workshop using authentic tools and timbers sawn in the mill.**

LEFT: The triangle can be heard around the park when the mill operator summons visitors for the demonstration. RIGHT TOP: The log is fed into the blade at 1/3 inch per stroke. RIGHT BOTTOM: This piece of the original saw blade was a key to reconstructing the mill.

The Mill

THE CENTERPIECE OF THE DEVELOPED PARK TODAY is the reconstructed, water-powered saw mill. Watching it saw boards is the highlight of a visit to Historic Mill Creek Discovery Park. When water is released and the flutter wheel begins to turn, the whole building shakes. As the saw and its frame move up and down up to 120 times a minute one can feel and see the power contained in the small creek.

Before the invention of steam engines, the most reliable source of power for operating simple machinery was to use falling water to turn wheels. Water wheels have blades or buckets on the outside rim. Flowing water strikes these and turns the wheels. The most common wheels were mounted vertically on a horizontal axle. The axle was connected to gears that operated the saws and millstones. Different types of wheels were used in mills. The type

1. crib; 2. flutter wheel; 3. crank; 4. pitman arm; 5. saw frame; 6. saw blade; 7. ratchet system; 8. rag wheel; 9. rag shaft; 10. carriage; 11. tub wheel; 12. lantern gear

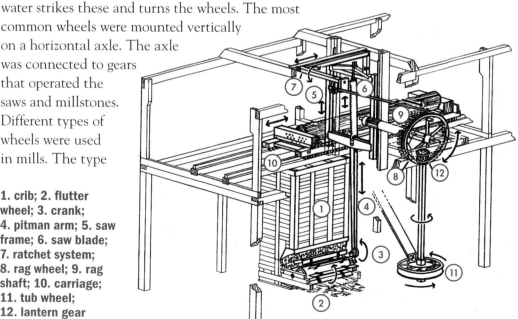

chosen depended upon the "head," the amount of water available and the speed and amount of power needed for the machine. The distance the water falls before striking the wheel is called the "head." The greater the head, the more power is made. Mill Creek's mill has a head of twelve feet.

The power comes not from the size of the creek but from the pressure of water held behind the dam. The water is directed from the mill pond, twelve feet above the water wheel, through a wooden sluice which empties into a large wooden box called a crib. A gate at the bottom of the crib is opened by the mill operator, and the water that gushes out falls with great weight on the flutter wheel, turning it. A flutter wheel is suitable for a mill with a lot of head. This small wheel provides a lot of power and speeds up to 120 revolutions per minute, a good choice for operating a saw. The flutter wheel is about four feet long and has 10 fins projecting from its sides. At the end of the flutter wheel is a crank, which is attached to a long wooden pole called a "pitman arm," because it does the same job that the "pit man" did when boards were sawn by hand. As the wheel and crank rotate, the pitman arm moves up and down and, being connected to the bottom of the saw frame, moves the saw blade up and down.

The mill also moves the log into the saw blade. A ratchet system attached to the top of the frame pushes against a large "rag wheel," slowly turning it and the "rag shaft" connected to it. Notches in the rag shaft push against large wooden teeth on the bottom of the carriage on which the log rests. Each up-and-down stroke of the saw blade moves the saw carriage and log into the blade one-third of an inch, cutting up to three

LEFT: **The reconstructed sawmill, based on careful historical and archaeological research, closely resembles Campbell's mill.**

feet of lumber a minute. The process sounds complicated, but when you watch it the process works smoothly, but noisily.

The mill contains a second wheel of a different design, called a tub wheel or turbine. Unlike other wheels, the tub wheel lays flat. It looks like a wagon wheel with slanted fins inside. It generates power by using both the speed and weight of the falling water hitting the slanted fins. It provides speed, but little power. By pulling a lever, the mill operator can engage the tub wheel to the rag wheel, putting the log carriage into reverse.

Although archaeologists never found the exact location of the sawmill at Mill Creek, they had a solid idea of what it looked like from a 1795 book by Oliver Evans, an inventive American millwright. The book, *The Young Millwright and Miller's Guide*, had detailed drawings and descriptions of an 18th-century mill. Architects were also greatly aided in their reconstruction by what they learned from examining the piece of original saw blade found at the site and from boards and stubshots cut in the mill that had been found in the 1825 Mission House on Mackinac Island. Marks on the boards showed the rake, or angle, of the saw blade and the set of the teeth. They also showed that the log advanced into the saw blade a 1/3 inch per stroke.

When work began on the reconstruction, however, no one had built a wa-ter-powered sawmill for more than a 100 years, and very few examples still existed. So, to be sure his plan would work, the designer built a scale model. The model, which worked perfectly, is now in the Visitor's Center museum.

The Power of Falling Water

Different types of wheels were used in mills. The type chosen depended upon the "head," the amount of water available and the speed and amount of power needed for the machine.

Undershot Wheel

Water shoots under the wheel. It is the oldest type of wheel and the least efficient.

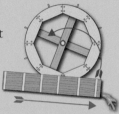

Breast Wheel

Water enters the side of the wheel. This was the most common type used in America. It is more efficient than an undershot but less efficient than an overshot.

Overshot Wheel

Water spills from above onto paddles to into buckets. A later innovation, it was much more efficient but more complicated to build and operate.

Tub Wheel

Unlike other wheels, this small wheel lays flat. It produces a lot of speed but little power.

Flutter Wheel

Water with a lot of "head" can turn this small but powerful wheel at high speeds.

Bibliography

Armour David A.

"Secrets of the Mill Creek mill…" in *Mackinac, the Gathering Place*, Russell McKee, editor. 1981. Michigan Natural Resources Magazine, Lansing.

Babb, Courtney et al.

"Mill Creek State Historic Park Wildlife Management Plan." 1993. Unpublished report.

Ford, Thomas B.

"Archaeological Investigations at the Mill Creek (Filbert) Site." 1979. Unpublished report.

"Archaeological Investigations at the Mill Creek (Filbert) Site." 1980. Unpublished report.

Heldman, Donald P.

"Reconstruction of the American Millwright's House (Structure 3) at Mill Creek Historic Park, Michigan." 1992. Unpublished report.

Hogg, Victor

Mill Creek an Interpretive Plan. 1977. Mackinac Island State Park Commission, Mackinac Island.

Kempton, Karen L.

"Archaeological Investigations at Old Mill Creek: An Early 19th Century Residence at the Straits of Mackinac." 1986. Unpublished M.A. thesis, Department of Anthropology, University of South Florida, Tampa.

Martin, Patrick E.

The Mill Creek Site and Pattern Recognition in Historical Archaeology. 1985. Archaeological Completion Report Series, Number 10. Mackinac Island State Park Commission, Mackinac Island.

Scott, Elizabeth M.

"Looking at Gender and More: Feminist Archaeology and a 19th Century Millwright's House." 1994. Unpublished paper.

Acknowledgments

- Graydon DeCamp
- William Fritz
- Lynn Morand
- Marlene Schmidt

- Jeffrey Dykehouse
- Jean McKenzie
- Victor R. Nelheibel
- Kay Stemkowski

Acknowledgments for Revised Edition

- Steven Brisson
- Jeffrey Dykehouse
- Lynn Morand Evans
- Dominick Miller
- Phil Porter

- Kathryn Cryderman
- Brenna Ehlke
- Brian Jaeschke
- Taylor Nash
- Keeney Swearer

Index

M

Mackinac Art Museum 1
Mackinac Associates 58
Mackinac Bridge 4
Mackinac Island 1, 3-4, 6, 33, 37-39, 43-44, 54, 62
Mackinac Island State Park 1
Mackinac Island State Park Commission 1, 30, 33-34, 49, 56
Mackinac State Historic Parks 1
Mackinaw State Forest 49
Martin, Patrick 33
Michigan 8, 11
Michigan Central Railroad 47
Michigan State University 33
Michilimackinac County 43
Mill Pond Trail 18, 20
Millwright's House 32, 45, 51, 54, 56, 58
Mission Church 43, 44
Mission House 44, 62
Myers Creek Mill 35
Myers, James 35

N

New York 38
North Central State Trail 48

O

Old Mackinac Point Lighthouse 1
Old Mackinaw Trail 48, 54
Olson, Ellis 30, 35, 49
Olson, Mary 30

P

Petoskey Lime Company 47
Port Huron 8

S

Saginaw Road 43
Scotland 37
Sounds of the Forest Discovery Station 18, 20
Stone, Lyle 30
Straits of Mackinac 1, 4, 6, 11, 17, 37
Sugar Shack Forest Trail 8, 20-21

T

Treaty of Greenville 40
Treetop Discovery Tower 3-4, 16-18

U

U.S. 23 48

Upper Great Lakes Regional Commission 56

V

Visitor's Center, David A. Armour 1-2, 4, 8, 18, 20, 23, 45, 56, 62, 68

W

War of 1812 30
Water Power Station 2
Watson, Walter 35
Wellington, Field Marshall 54
Wendell, William W. 47
World's Columbian Exposition 35

About the Author

DAVID A. ARMOUR (1937-2010) served as Deputy Director of the Mackinac Island State Park Commission from 1967 until 2003. The David A. Armour Visitor's Center was named after him in 2008 in recognition of his many years of service to the commission.

A native of Grove City, Pennsylvania, he was a graduate of Calvin College (B.A. 1959) and Northwestern University (M.A. 1960 and Ph.D. 1965). While teaching at the University of Wisconsin-Milwaukee he went to work at Mackinac during the summers of 1965 and 1966.

Author of numerous books and articles, he shared Mackinac with his wife, Grace, and their four children, Marian, Arthur, David, and Anneke, who grew up and worked on Mackinac Island.